MICHAEL E. MIRANDA
COLLECTIONS CONSULTANTS

THE ART OF TELEPHONE DEBT COLLECTIONS

1

COLLECTIONS CONSULTANTS

THE COMPANY THAT BRINGS SOLID SOLUTIONS
TO YOUR ACCOUNTS RECEIVABLES PROBLEMS

© Collections Consultants
P.O. Box 181441
Arlington, Texas 76096
collectionsconsultants.com

INTRODUCTION

You are a Professional Debt-Collector with an important service to offer. Professional Debt-Collectors stimulate the flow of stagnated dollars frozen due to unpaid bills. Professional Debt-Collectors move billions of **dollars** yearly, pumping **money** back into our economy thereby strengthening our financial system. .

Your position as a Professional Debt-Collector charges you with the responsibility of guiding the debtor towards the goal of paying debts owed to the company you work for or represent. By doing this you stimulate cash flow and contribute to the profitability of the company you are employed by and in turn strengthen our economy.

While there might be many people who harbor a negative image of the debt-collection profession, the company you work for or represent has elected to hire you to make recovery of these bad debts on their behalf. Your job then is to make every reasonable and legal effort to successfully collect on these debts or delinquent accounts while bringing credit to yourself and satisfaction to the company you work for. .

This book will cover how to collect these delinquent accounts using one of the most efficient tools possible there are for this task, **The Telephone.**

The material presented in this booklet will provide you with the tools, skills and insight to be successful in your mission of collecting these delinquent accounts.

This book will cover:

- The Debt-Collections Profession and how it effects our economy
- The importance of your role in today's economy
- The reluctant relationship between the Debtor and the Debt-Collector.

- Maslow's Hierarchy of Psychological Need Stages
- The Eight Step Collection Call in Detail
- How to create a debtor profile to enhance your ability to provide a helpful service to them.
- How to define and apply the three appeals to collect money from the debtor
- Identify the barriers that prevent success at each phase of the collection process and

- Create solutions to overcome them
- Exercises that will help you to practice or, in the seminar, role-play actual collection calls thereby building confidence with the tools you have acquired while honing the skills you have learned.
- How to set performance goals to achieve your's and your company's or client's desired results.

8

- Techniques on setting and achieving your own personal goals.

#1

THE DEBT COLLECTION PROFESSION INDUSTRY

Regardless of what one believes about the Debt-Collection-Profession you can not deny the industry's necessity to the international economy. This section will cover the breadth and depth of this industry and the impact that bad debts have on the financial system. It will show the importance of the Professional-Debt-Collector not only to this industry but to the whole economy as well plus identify the key sectors of the credit and debt-collections industry or what is now to being referred to by many as the Accounts Receivable Management Industry or ARM.

Our economic system should be simple. The consumer buys a product or service then pays for it and that's it. Works great but this idea breaks down very quickly when the consumer desires or even needs to purchase something that cost's more money than he has at the time. Credit grantors fill this need by providing loans to finance these purchases. The consumer repays the loan over a contractually agreed upon time. When the consumer, for whatever reason, fails to live up to that contractual agreement bad debt is created.

This bad debt has a considerable impact on the economy.

For example, in 2007 the total US consumer debt (which includes installment debt, but not mortgage debt) reached **$2.46 Trillion dollars**. The exact figures were not available at the time of this writing but on average the amount of debt placed for collection each year is around 30% to 35% which would be approximately **$738-billion dollars to $861-billion dollars** placed for collection in 2007. Again the exact figures were not available at this writing but the ARM Industry successfully recovers an average of around 15% of the debt placed with them which means that approximately **$110-billion,700-millon to $129-billion,150-million dollars** is what was actually collected. Leaving somewhere between **$627-billion,300-million dollars and $731-billion,185-million dollars** worth of bad debt uncollected. Resulting in a cost that year of between **$2,100.00 and $2,500.00** for each and every person in the United States.

Obviously the Debt-Collection industry has a significant place in our economy. Let's look at the different areas or industries for which and by which money is collected.

- Medical: A major source of Paper for 3rd party collection agencies.
- Telecommunications:
- Retail:
- Checks: Since the advent of debit cards the use of checks and the number of bad checks has dropped tremendously.
- Retail Credit Cards:
- Commercial (Business to Business):
- Banks:

- Credit Unions:
- Student Loans:
- And lastly, the Original Creditor (First-Party):

As a Professional-Debt-Collector knowledge of the details behind the accounts that you collect on is critical for success. Good product knowledge is essential. You must know all the ins and outs of the product that your company or the company you represent sells. At times this product knowledge is precisely what will give you the edge when dealing with debtors. The debtor's excuses for non payment are much more easily answered and overcome when your product knowledge is sufficiently good enough that you are able to readily remind the debtor of the value of the product or service they obtained from or through your company on credit. Study your company's or client's products and services. Learn all of their product's benefits. Knowing what these benefits are will enable you to explain the product or service in detail when demanding payment from the debtor. It also helps you to anticipate the objections and stalls that the debtor might attempt to use when confronted with the debt.

In this section we have found that Bad debt, while not only contributing to billions of lost dollars each year also makes a significant impact on our national economy as well as the international economy. The role of the <u>Professional-Debt-Collector</u> is not only a necessary part of almost any business but is vital to the overall health of our economy as a whole.

Debtors who do not or are not able to uphold their end of the economic bargain create hardship for us all. Merchants and service providers are forced to increase their prices to offset to offset the losses caused by delinquent payments, creating an unnecessary burden for the majority of the population.

#2

COLLECTOR & DEBTOR A RELUCTANT RELATIONSHIP

Debtors have qualities that can make them financially successful or unsuccessful. As a Professional-Debt-Collector you also have qualities that can bring success as well as disappointment. We all have many qualities and skills to draw from that would enable us to obtain payment in full from the debtor. Among them are intelligence, personality and of course our ability to use the telephone. Combining theses qualities and skills with psychology, knowledge and inspiration allows the professional debt-collector to have the edge in this reluctant relationship we have with the debtor. This section will help you to understand how to use these qualities and skills so that you can better service your company and the debtor.

In this section we will

- Define the characteristics of the successful Professional-Debt-Collector

- Classify the four categories of consumer debt
- Apply a psychological model to identify the debtor's needs
- Identify three affective appeals to encourage the debtor to pay the debt.

The successful
Professional-Debt Collector,

- is informed about the credit/collection industry,
- can use a wide variety of collection techniques

- is knowledgeable about the company's product or services that he or she collects on.

The foundation of any successful Professional-Debt-Collector begins with a positive self image. They have a strong belief in self, are prepared and possess a Positive Mental Attitude or PMA.

For an exercise, write down and then answer the following questions.

1. What ways can I cultivate a strong belief in myself.
2. What ways can I be better prepared
3. What ways can I create a Positive Mental Attitude or PMA in myself.

There are specific areas that will undoubtedly improve your collection results, with a PMA being perhaps the most important.

There are certain qualities that, by having an awareness of and developing to their fullest, will definitely improve your odds of becoming a successful Professional-Debt-Collector.

These qualities are

- Accuracy
- Alertness
- Attentiveness
- A businesslike attitude
- Staying composed
- Being decisive
- Being dependable

- Staying detached
- Flexibility
- Being goal oriented
- Imaginativeness
- Inquisitiveness
- Interest in your profession
- Being logical
- Maturity
- Staying motivated
- Being observant
- Resourcefulness
- Sales-Mindedness
- Tactfulness
- Having an understanding attitude

For an exercise, on a piece of paper make 3 columns. In column one list which of the qualities you think you just naturally possess. In column two list which of these qualities you think you naturally possess but need to develop through coaching and further training. Then in column three list which of these qualities you feel you do not naturally possess in any capacity what so ever. Keep this piece of paper then later discuss each of your choices with your supervisor or a colleague and decide if each choice is a quality you should develop and how will you go about developing it.

Besides a positive self-image, successful debt-collectors have qualities that offer additional advantages over less successful debt-collectors. These qualities manifest themselves in different ways such as posture, work-space and the very words the debt-collector uses. These words are reflective of one's attitude in general. Success looks and sounds very distinctive.

Read and decide which of the following examples or phrases reflects an attitude of a successful debt-collector and a, not so successful debt-collector.

- **Unsuccessful;** I do not have time to accomplish everything.
- **Successful;** In the morning I'll work my calls then after lunch I'll set a plan for tomorrow.

- **Unsuccessful;** I only have a hour left then I can go home.
- **<u>Successful</u>;** It's getting close to the time that people are home. I'll be able to meet my contact goals

- **Unsuccessful;** I hope I can get some people to pay today
- **<u>Successful</u>;** I'm going to get at least eight immediate payments today.

- **Unsuccessful;** I'm just going to start calling and see what happens.
- **<u>Successful</u>;** I have the eight steps here and some objections. I'm working the three payments-late accounts today so I know there will be some financial problems involved but I'm prepared.

Now that you have a snapshot of what makes a debt-collector successful, lets move on to the other part of the relationship, the debtor.

Successful debt-collectors gather as much information as possible about a debtor before attempting to contact them. The more information gathered the easier it becomes to collect the money owed. One source of general information is the National Foundation Of Consumer Credit (NFCC). This organization has constructed a profile composite of the debtors being served by Credit Counseling Services across the nation. They found that the average debtor serviced by these

Credit Counseling Services has the following characteristics;

- Approximately 37-years of age.
- 46% are male
- 54% are female
- 35% are single never been married
- 46% are Married
- 19% are separated, divorced or widowed
- There are 2.8 people per family
- Average annual gross income is $29,425.00
- Average total debt is $23,184.00
- The average number of creditors is 10

Now that you have the typical debtor statistics the next piece of the puzzle is to understand just what it is that causes people to have debt. Are they careful, careless or criminal? There are many causes for people finding themselves in debt. They can be best grouped into four categories of delinquency.

1. **Circumstantial;** These debtors are unable to handle their obligations due to life occurrences such as loss of job, change in marital status, natural disaster, sickness or personal injury.

2. **Emotional;** These debtors believe that they just deserve the service or merchandise they have purchased, even though they are not able to afford it. Normally their style of living is way beyond their means or income.
3. **Intellectual;** These debtors usually have the means to pay their debt but are unable to budget their income. They don't keep clear financial records and might have little idea about their financial situation.

4. **Criminal Intent;** These debtors are actually credit criminals. They use fraud and deceit to receive goods and services for which they never intend to pay for.

Let's consider some tough collection situations and based on what we have learned so far determine what category you would most likely classify these situations and then how you would handle them.

- ***"I don't have a job"***
- <u>Circumstantial</u> Ask the debtor why they are out of work and have they applied for or are they collecting on their unemployment. Probe the debtor for any other sources of income or money they might have and you could even renegotiate their payment amount if that is feasible or possible.

- ***"Things will be better next month. I'll pay then."***
- Emotional Get specific payment information such as the precise date the debtor will pay, the exact amount the debtor will be paying and particularly by what means they will be paying. Attempt to get post dated checks and or check by phones for the payment.

- ***"I never realized that a bounced check could cost me this much."***
- Intellectual Get the debtor to replace the returned item then probe for the number or the amount of their other debts and for any other sources of income.

- ***"I have insurance that covers that. I have never NOT paid my bills"***

- Circumstantial and Intellectual and Emotional This one is simple. Explain clearly but politely so the debtor understands that regardless of any insurance coverage they might have it is still their contractual responsibility to make certain that the debt is paid.

- ***"I'll pay when I feel like it and you can't force me to pay."***

- Emotional Stay cool and calm. You must keep control of the situation. Reinforce the idea that you're attempting to help them resolve the problem and not trying to force them to do anything.

- ***I am no longer married to that person."***

- <u>Circumstantial</u> If this person is still legally responsible for the debt then politely explain their contractual obligation and continue collection efforts. If they are not then probe for any and all information you can get regarding the debtor.

- ***"I have filed for bankruptcy"***
- <u>Circumstantial</u> Get the attorney's name and number and end the

call. Federal law is very specific about contacting a debtor while they are in bankruptcy. Call the attorney for the bankruptcy information. The debt does remain open for collection efforts to continue until the bankruptcy is actually filed and you have a case number.

- ***"I know I promised to pay the whole thing but I needed that money for some other things.***

Isn't something better than nothing?"

- Emotional and Circumstantial

Whatever the amount paid, thank the debtor for their payment but also stress to debtor the need to pay the full payment each month. Set up a better and more acceptable but specific payment arrangement.

- ***"I sent in my payment. It must have gotten lost in the mail."***
- Circumstantial Politely get specific payment information such as the exact amount sent and the date it was sent. Identify how it was sent (overnight, certified, regular mail etc.) and any other pertinent information. Attempt to get an additional payment now. Then, and this is important, be sure to follow up on the payment that was supposedly mailed.

- ***"How many times do I have to tell you people? He is not at home"*** *or* ***"He does not live here."***
- <u>Emotional and or Criminal Intent</u>
  Now this could be criminal intent if the person is lying but it could also be an emotional response if the person is feeling frustrated at receiving numerous collection calls for the debtor. There is not a lot you can do in this case, attempt to get any additional

information on the debtor then leave a message for the debtor and continue collection efforts.

- ***"That person is deceased"***
- <u>Circumstantial</u> Get the estate information and if possible continue collection efforts on the estate. If an attorney is representing the estate then unless told specifically otherwise you will need to restrict all contact to the attorney.

Next, we now come to the Maslow Model.

Abraham Maslow (1908-1970) was an American psychologist who studied human motivation. His research and findings have turned out to be very helpful to the debt-collection industry for a number of reasons. The most important of which is Maslow's discovery that all human beings operate in the same manner when it comes to satisfying the need for what they want.

We as debt-collectors rely on this premise when trying to understand the debtor's situation or what has truly caused the debtor to be in debt. We are then able to effectively formulate appeals by applying the Maslow model. We do this by first determining
which of **<u>Maslow's Hierarchy of Psychological Need Stages</u>** that the debtor is operating in.

The Maslow Hierarchy model consists of five psychological need stages.

The **first** one is **Self Fulfillment**, this debtor's attitude most likely would be one that they might say or think something like ***"I can't concern myself with this"*** These tend to be people who have the money but just forget to pay their bills because they're always to busy.

The **second** need stage is **Esteem**, this debtor's attitude is such that he or she might say or think something like ***"How dare you call me about a bill"*** These debtors tend to be self confident with a large ego. They want to be in control and always try to get in the last word.

The **third** psychological need stage is **Social**, This debtors attitude might have them saying or thinking ***"Who else knows about this"?*** These debtors are very concerned over what other people think of them and will always keep up with other people's names. They seem to use credit freely and are normally hard to contact. They will tend to make up a high percentage of your dodgers.

The **fourth** psychological need stage is **Security**, This debtor's attitude might result in them saying or thinking ***"How is this going to affect my credit"*** These are people who want a sure thing. They are generally employed, have savings that they don't touch and tend to have credit cards they don't use.

The ***fifth*** and final psychological need stage is **Physical**, This debtor's attitude would be such that they could think or you might hear them say ***"I can't pay this now, my rent is due."*** This is probably the most difficult psychological need stage to collect

from. Their food, water, shelter and health will always come first. These debtors tend to live from check to check struggling to support their family with no savings at all.

(1)Self –fulfillment

The "Maslow" Model

(2)Esteem

----

(3)Social

----

(4)Security

----

(5)Physical

Once we understand **Maslow's Hierarchy of Psychological Need Stages** we next must look at what debtor appeals we might use to collect the money that is owed. There are three basic debtor appeals, **Honesty**, **Pride**, and **Anxiety**. When these are used in conjunction with Maslow's Hierarchy of Psychological Need Stages they can become the single best way to inspire debtors to pay what they owe.

For further explanation let's start with **Honesty**. Most people are brought up that honesty is a good thing. You can use this appeal with debtors who are displaying the **Social** and or the **Esteem** psychological need stages. For example you might politely remind the debtor that it is not in their best interest to and they really do not want to, go back on their original agreement and then set up an agreeably feasible payment arrangement with that debtor.

The next appeal to discuss is **Pride**. Pride is by far one of the strongest motivational forces there are. This appeal can be used with the **Social**, **Esteem** and or the **Self-Fulfillment** psychological need stages. You would want to use very affirming language with these debtors. Mention the things that you feel the debtor would approve of. You would need to offer these debtors particularly sound payment arrangements.

The last of the debtor appeals to discuss is **Anxiety**; Believe it or not this is a stronger motivational force than even **Pride**. This appeal seems to work best with the **Security** psychological need stage but in certain cases it can also work with the **Physical** psychological need stage. Here you can explain the ramifications of non-payment, the negative side of not paying what they owe. You do not want to sound menacing to the debtor though and you never want to threaten an action that your company does not do or does not intend to do as you could violate the **FDACP** laws if you do so be careful. What you would want to do next is show them a light at the end of the tunnel so to speak by offering an affordable payment arrangement.

To summarize; Debt-collectors are critical to the health of the economy. However there aren't too many debtors who are looking forward to receiving a call from a Professional-Debt-Collector.

When debtors renege on their agreement they made with your company or your client's company the creditor, the Professional-Debt-Collector and the debtor are thrown into a reluctant relationship.

Your personal and professional attributes are the strength behind your success. When you rely on your intellect, trust your abilities and use the knowledge you now have of the five **Maslow Psychological Need Stages** in conjunction with the three appeals outlined in this section the odds are increased tremendously in your favor that your collection efforts will be successful.

#3

THE EIGHT STEP TELEPHONE DEBT-COLLECTION CALL.

We now come to section three where we will discuss the **Eight-Step-Telephone-Debt-Collection-Call**.

You, the Professional-Telephone-Debt-Collector, are the heart of your debt-collection team. Although the managers, skip-tracers, and clerical staff are working towards the same goal, it is you the Professional-Debt-Collector that actually speaks with the debtor. It is you the Professional-Debt-Collector that sells the debtor on paying the debt. So be consistent in your efforts. Successful Professional-Debt-Collectors realize that a consistent approach makes even the most difficult calls more manageable.

In this section we will explore the eight steps of every debt-collection call. By understanding these eight steps and following this call model you'll find that your debt-collection calls will be much more successful.

By the end of this section you will be able to identify each of the eight steps that comprise a successful debt-collection call. You will be able to recognize the barriers that can occur at each step of this debt-collection call model and create solutions to overcome them.

Preparing For the Call

Because in this day and time successful debt-collections means communicating with as many debtors as possible in the time available, a little preparation can go a long way. So in preparing for the call, you will first want to check the debtor's payment record. If the account is new to you it will provide you with needed background information, if you have previously worked the account this will refresh your memory of what you did and said previously.

Next, you need to look at the debtor's responses to past debt-collection actions. You will want to know when the last call was made, the reason for the previous call and the outcome of all the previous calls made in the last thirty days.

Next, you can plan your strategy. You need to know what benefits you can offer the debtor to pay in full or bring the account fully up to date today. You should also decide just how quickly you want this particular account to be paid if the debtor in not able to pay today.

Next, you must determine your bottom line. Determine what is the lowest PMT-amount you are able take or are willing to accept, what is the latest date you want or need the account to be paid in full or paid up to date by and what options are you willing or able to offer the debtor to achieve that bottom line goal.

Lastly, you need to prepare your questions. Remember these questions are to achieve only one goal and that is obtaining meaningful information.

One more thing, this whole process should take you no more than fifteen to thirty seconds or less.

Now let's take a closer look at the process itself. You make a single call yet there can be so many dimensions to that call. A standard debt-collection call might normally consist of eight steps however, depending upon the situation, you might use all the steps or you might use only some of the steps. You might even repeat one or two of the steps several times before the call is completed and payment is actually obtained. Each debt-collection call is different.

Before we go any further let us also remember that your voice is the main way you communicate in this process. When you talk to someone in person they hear what you say but they are also picking up on visual cues such as body language. When you are talking to a debtor on the phone there are no visual cues. Your voice and the tone of your voice take the place of body language. So when you start to actually make the call you want to be sure your voice is clear, unhurried, audible and calm.

The-Eight-Step-

Debt-Collection

Telephone-Call

1. StepOne,

Identify the debtor. You dial the number you are calling on the telephone, it rings and someone answers. You must now first and foremost determine if you are speaking to the debtor or not. Per the **F**air-**D**ebt-and-**C**ollection-**P**ractices-**A**ct or **FDCPA**, originally enacted in 1978, you may only speak to the debtor or the debtor's spouse. One way to insure that you are talking to the correct person is to first ask for the debtor by their first name only. Lets say the debtor's name is Bill Debtor, you would ask "Is Bill there" if the person says for instance "This is Bill" Then you would say "Bill Debtor"? or "Mr. Debtor"? and wait for him to affirm. If the debtor is a minor you may speak with the debtor's legal guardian but you have to first know who the minor's legal guardian is and then you have to determine that the person you are speaking to is that legal guardian just like you have to do with the debtor. If the debtor has an attorney representing them in this matter then you may speak with the debtor's attorney. If you have received a letter of representation from the debtor's attorney then you should be calling their attorney and must speak only with their attorney. Or at least you must have made a reasonable attempt to speak with the debtor's attorney. Anyone who has dealt with attorneys knows how difficult it can be at times to get a debtor's attorney to take your phone call. If you have made a reasonable number of attempts to contact the debtor's attorney and the attorney has not accepted your calls or has not returned your calls then and only then can you go back to contacting the debtor direct. Other than that you may not speak to any other third party regarding the debt unless you have specific permission from the debtor to speak to that particular person preferably in writing.

2. StepTwo,

Identify yourself. Once you have identified the debtor, you know you are talking to the correct person, you then must identify yourself. In doing so you must give your correct name and the name of the company you represent or work for. Again, per the FDCPA, you may not give a fake name, or a fake company name. You may not allude to be something you are not such as an attorney or from the "legal department" for example, if you are not. You must be honest in giving out your name or more importantly your company's name and your position with said company. Essentially, per the **FDCPA**, you may not lie to the debtor at all.

3. **3.** StepThree,

Request payment in full. Your goal is to achieve payment in full without having to contact the debtor again. Some refer to this as the one call close. Depending on the situation it doesn't necessarily mean that the money must be in the office immediately, but it does mean that the debtor has made a firm promise to pay in full on or by a specific date. You might even take the perspective of determining how much time the company or the debtor needs to pay rather than how much money the debtor can pay now. So at this point you simply state the purpose of your call and politely request payment in full. Just by initially requesting the total amount due be paid in full each and every time you contact a debtor, you will increase your debt-collection efforts. There will always be a certain percentage of debtors that will pay the total amount due just because you requested it. It also then gives you a base for further negotiations toward a reasonable payment-arrangement should the debtor not be able to pay in full. Please remember, per the

FDCPA, you may not be abusive or threatening.

4. StepFour, ***The-Psychological-Pause***.

Successful debt-collectors recognize the power of silence and always employ the **Psychological-Pause**. The **Psychological-Pause** is one of the most powerful parts of a profitable or successful debt-collection call. So after you have stated the purpose of your call and have made your request for payment in full you then pause and when I say wait I mean wait, wait for the debtor to respond no matter how long it seams to take for the debtor to respond, say nothing just wait. This is critical part of the call. The debtor is thinking of an appropriate reply and it is when the debtor is most likely to tell you what you need to know so you can possibly negotiate the debtor's payment in full. If not all at once then at least with a reasonable payment-arrangement.

The debtor's reaction to your request for payment in full, after you've employed the **Psychological-Pause**, depends largely on the cause of the debt. There are three basic reactions that you will get from the debtor.

- The **first** possible reaction, and of course the most preferable, is the debtor simply makes payment to you for what is owed or due at the time upon your request for payment.

- The **second** possible reaction is the **Stall**. When the debtor offers excuses for not paying. At this point in the conversation you should recall and employ the four causes of delinquency, **Circumstantial**, **Emotional**, **Intellectual** and **Criminal-Intent**. If the debtor is stalling then remember a stall is normally not the real reason why the debtor isn't paying so you might have to probe some for additional information.

- The **third** possible reaction is an **Objection**. It deals directly with the payment and why the debtor will not pay. Again refer to and employ the four causes of delinquency

Circumstantial, **Emotional**, **Intellectual** and **Criminal-Intent**. Remember an Objection can also be a legitimate dispute by the debtor so listen carefully and closely to what the debtor is saying.

Let's take a look at identifying Stalls and Objections because if you don't respond to a Stall or Objection correctly you are giving the debtor more time to think about avoiding the debt. If not handled correctly the result could be a call that ends without having the opportunity to question the debtor, work out payment now or set a reasonable payment-arrangement.

Now how does one know when it's an attempt to buy time or if it really is a situation that you can not have an affect on? Well it's quite simple, you can tell by just knowing the difference and listening to what the debtor has to say.

Here listed, are some examples. Are their responses a Stall or an Objection?

- Debtor says, "I never received that merchandise."
  - **Objection**

- Debtor says, "I'm not paying that finance charge (or late fee)."
  - **Stall**

- Debtor says, “I have already paid this or I sent this payment in already”
  - **Could be an Objection or a Stall**

- Debtor says, “I’m not responsible for what my wife bought”
  - **Stall**

- Debtor says, "This isn't a good time. Can I call you back (or can you call me back)."
  - **<u>Stall</u>**

- Debtor says, "The work was never finished. I won't pay until the job is done."
  - **<u>Objection</u>**

- Debtor says, "I have insurance to cover that."
  - **<u>Stall</u>**

It is simply amazing that you are able to garner all that information by employing a simple **Psychological-Pause**. Now all of this that you have gone through with the debtor after employing that **Psychological-Pause** will now enable you to take the next step.

5. StepFive,

Determine the Problem. Up to this point as you have gone through steps one through four of the call certainly you have realized that the debtor has some sort of situation or problem that is preventing him from paying on the debt. Otherwise the debtor would not be delinquent. A close examination of the exact reasons why the debt is not being paid will help you proceed in collecting on the account. It is up to you to determine what the problem is. How do you do that? By asking probing questions. Is the debtor working. Have they lost their job or been injured preventing them from work? Are they recently separated or divorced? What other expenses do they have that could be preventing them from paying? These are just a few examples of numerous possible questions but once you have determined the problem it is now time for the next step. You have made your request for payment in full, used the **Psychological-Pause**, asked probing questions after which the debtor has responded with the real reason the debt hasn't been paid and you have determined the problem so it is now time to employ step six.

6. StepSix,

Determining the Solution.

Regardless of the reason or excuse given you to you by the debtor, you must convince the debtor that they want to pay the debt. This is where the use of the **Three Debtor-Appeals** come into play, formulate your negotiation to appeal to the debtor's sense of **Honesty**, **Pride** and or **Anxiety**. It is then up to you to help the debtor find a solution that will enable the debtor to pay. That is your job. So by this point in the call you should have determined **two things**, **one**; what, if anything, is the debtor objecting to and, **two**; what are the points that you both agree on. Once you have determined the solution you are now ready to work out an agreement on the objections.

Before we go any further lets talk about Negotiation. Negotiation is the process you will use to overcome or solve a problem so you can reach a desired goal. In the majority of debt-collection calls you will enter into some form of negotiation with the debtor in order to obtain payment on the account. We are going to briefly look at four negotiation techniques and how you might use them.

- **First**; Know Your Company's Products or Business. Be familiar with the account you are working, the type of debtor with whom you are working including the debtor's financial restraints and the various money sources available.

- **Second**, Establish Issues of Agreement. Try to identify the statements made that the debtor does not dispute.
- **Third**, Verify the Facts, Verify the facts of the debt. Discover things the debtor won't acknowledge. For these areas of disagreement form the basis of the 4th-technique.
- **Fourth**, Discover the Issues of Disagreement. Once you have verified the facts you

will discover the issues with which the debtor does not agree. You now have the information you need to negotiate a solution.

Let’s now look at some additional negotiation strategies. Many of the strategies and techniques during the negotiation process are those that you would normally use during a debt-collection call.

The most effective negotiation results when you

- Place yourself in a leadership position and control the conversation.
- Discover as much as you can about the debtor you are calling.
- Show a genuine interest in understanding the debtor.
- Maintain an organized and focused approach
- Stick to the subject at hand

- Use specifics in your requests and statements
- Speak in simple and easy to understand language
- Avoid the use of critical or offensive words
- Use the Psychological-Pause and recognize the value of silence.

Now is where the use of the Debtor-Appeals come into play.

7. Step Seven ***Close The Deal***.

Once you have an agreement, Close The Deal. Do not end the call until you've accomplished the following **three things**.

- **One**; Agree on a definite date and a definite method for payment
- **Two**; Get the Debtor's agreement on the precise and specific directions for remitting the payment. **Three**; Stress to the debtor the

importance of complying with your agreement.

8. StepEight simple but very important.

Update the Debtor's File. It is critical to keep thorough written records of all debtor contacts and conversations time, date, and the results of your last contact. Record in detail how payments are to be made, the amounts, the method and exactly when they are due to be sent and or received. Your documentation should include any information source, whether you have spoken with the debtor, spouse, friends or the employer. Identify that person by specific name plus position and include that in the debtor's file also.

To summarize, remember that two way communications is vital to the debt-collection process. Because your initial goal is payment in full on the first call your best approach is to use the telephone and adhere to a communication system that is both deliberate and focused. Plan your call by quickly researching the account.

Then move on to the eight steps of the debt-collection call.

1. **Identify the Debtor**

2. **Identify Yourself**

3. **Request Payment In Full**

4. **Psychological-Pause**

5. **Determine the Problem**

6. **Determine the Solution**

7. **Close the Deal**

8. **Update the Debtor's Files**

#4 BUILDING WITH THE TOOLS

Now that we have the tools to work with we can begin building our approach. In this section we will discuss actual calls. You can at this point get with another coworker and roll play a debt-collection call with each other. We will apply the information and the models covered earlier in the book.

At the conclusion of this section you should have improved your skill at identifying the debtor's cause of debt and be able to apply Maslow's Psychological Need Stages Hierarchy to every debt-collection call and formulate an effective payment appeal.

#4 / Building With the Tools

- **Cause of Debt:** ______________________

- **Maslow Stage:** ______________________

Appeal To: ______________________

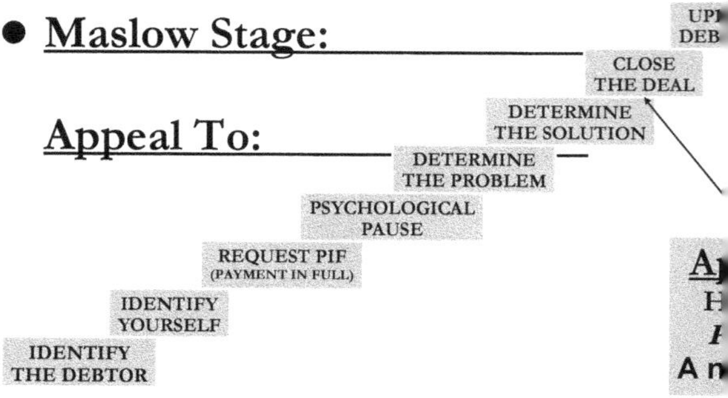

In order to assist the debtor in paying the debt you should believe that the debtor does owe the debt and that the debtor will pay the debt. Then you can move on to your tools and always

- Know all about the product or service that the debt is owe for.
- Learn the debtor's cause for delinquency.
- Question and probe to discover the debtor's Psychological needs.

Remember that no two calls are the same or alike. You will not be able to completely script the debt-collection call so that you can always achieve payment in full. If you come prepared and have a strong knowledge base, you will greatly increase your chances of success.

•

#5 READY, SET, GOAL

What's next?

Pinpoint the concepts of this book that you can use immediately then set yourself goals to get results. Your job performance will be improved when you take the time to examine the things you are doing well and apply ideas on improving the things on which you aren't.

By the end of this section you should understand the value of goal setting to the successful debt-collector. You should be able to identify at least 3 performance-enhancing ideas that you can immediately apply upon returning to your work station. You should be able to write down short-term and long-term goals that will support those goals of the company you work for and positively impact your role as a debt-collector.

Goal Setting

Setting goals will help you to be successful. Goals will inspire you, outline a course of action to take, help you gain pride in your work and show you exactly where you're going and the progress you are making.

Goals that are in agreement with the goals set by your company are exponentially easier to reach. By setting goals for yourself that agree with your company, not only will you have the resources you need but most importantly you will have your company's support.

Setting Priorities

Setting priorities equals success. Before you set goals, look at what you need to accomplish in your current role as a debt-collector. Your supervisor assuredly has performance expectations of you. Use those expectations as your foundation and shape your activities so you can easily achieve both personal and professional satisfaction. Priorities force you to ask and answer necessary questions before you set your goals. When deciding if an event should be a priority, ask yourself the following

- How urgent is it?
- How often must it be done?
- Can someone else do it more effectively than I can?
- Is it part of a larger company picture or effort to which I am committed?
- What will happen if this item is not done at all?

Establishing Priorities

- Helps you determine how your time is spent.
- Relieves the stress of feeling overwhelmed.
- Give focus when you're faced with "now what".

When setting goals remember to

- Be realistic
- Write your goals down
- Describe reaching each goal
- Keep your goals consistent with those of the company you're employed by.
- Make goals interesting and challenge yourself.
- Review and update your goals regularly.

Remember, this is important so especially remember, Develop a plan and then Work your plan. I'll say it again. Develop a plan and then <u>Work your plan.</u>

For example, goals that every debt-collector might want are

- I will collect more dollars
- I will improve my recovery percentage
- I will increase my debtor contacts
- I will reduce the time spent with each debtor.

Goals help focus your efforts and give your life direction. Goals can be created for every aspect of your personal and professional life. They are most effective when they are integrated into a unified whole.

As a professional debt-collector your primary goal should be payment in full. You will also benefit when you make a promise that you will collect more dollars, improve your recovery percentage, increase your debtor contact, reduce the time spent with each debtor and as a consequence get fewer broken arrangements.

More than anything, when you decide what you want to accomplish remember you will be most effective when your aims align with those of you company's organizational plan.

Be the best Professional-Debt-Collector you can be.

THE END

www.ingramcontent.com/pod-product-compliance
Lightning Source LLC
Chambersburg PA
CBHW070407200326
41518CB00011B/2105

* 9 7 8 0 5 7 8 0 1 1 9 7 4 *